AF561708
I
AM
HONEST
A Coloring Book For Girls & Boys

Published By: SketchBuddies®

ISBN: 978-81-941108-5-9

Hey... Thank You for being AWESOME!
We hope that you have a fun time with your book. We have a gift for you. You can download a free printable set of our best coloring pages by visiting our website :
SketchBuddies.com
It would be so cool if you could share your completed images with us. You can find us on f / @vrSketchBuddies &
on @vr_SketchBuddies.
We are always working hard to improve our books. Please let us know how we are doing by writing a review of our book on your favorite online book store.
You can always reach out to us on social media. #vrSketchBuddies

My name is ____________

Stick Your
Picture Here

My Superpower is
I am truthful in what I say and do
I AM HONEST
H

People can
TRUST me

I am Honest
with
Everybody,
Everyday

I say the Truth even if
I think I will get in trouble
because
I Am Brave

A
A
I never make up rumours
or
Share rumours with others

I do
what is
Right
regardless
of who is
around

I never
cheat or steal
from others

I am never
afraid to speak
the TRUTH

People Respect Me
because
I am Honest

I
always
follow
the
RULES

I always keep
my Promise

I never hide
the TRUTH

I am Honest
even when it
is difficult
1
2
3

I don't take things
that don't belong to me

If I want something
I always ask for it

I always take
Responsibility
for my actions
Happy
BirthDay!

I never
exaggerate
the facts

I am Honest
with my friends
whenever we play

I always tell the truth
even if I think
I will lose

I help my Friends
to tell the Truth

If I make a mistake,
I say 'I am Sorry'
and tell the Truth
B
C
A
C
A
B

I tell the truth when
my teacher asks me
anything
1

I admit
when I am
Wrong

I always
Play by the Rules

Being Honest in my Heart
feels better than
Ice Cream

Honesty
is the
Best
Policy

I
AM
HONEST

I ♥ MOM
1
Being Honest
is CooL

When I am Honest with people, they ______________________

______________________

______________________

______________________

______________________

______________________

______________________

______________________

______________________

______________________

I like to tell the Truth
because

www.ingramcontent.com/pod-product-compliance
Lightning Source LLC
LaVergne TN
LVHW070400230826
846093LV00017B/548

* 9 7 8 8 1 9 4 1 1 0 8 5 9 *